You Are All Unique, Just Like Everybody Else

(I couldn't make this stuff up)

Suretta Williams

You Are All Unique, Just Like Everybody Else

(I couldn't make this stuff up)

Dedication

This book is dedicated to a very special person. Together we've shared stories, witnessed stressful situations, comforted hurt limbs, and driven to doctors' offices, hospital emergency rooms, and car accident scenes.

Alone she's chauffeured to and from scout meetings, camp, events, medical and dental appointments, and anywhere three growing kids needed to go.

We even drove three-and-a-half hours to surprise our son at an awards banquet (at the request of his teacher). While we've handled routine (and not-so-routine) teenage rites of passages and delighted in many accomplishments, we've also mourned and comforted failures when necessary.

Lastly, we've attended grammar school, middle school, high school, and college graduations and still have a few in our future.

Our next expectations are marriages and grandbabies, hopefully in that order. We don't even have a guess as to which child will be the first to meet this tall order, although I truly hope it isn't for a while; I'm too young (and feel too old) to be a grandmother.

Special Thanks

To a dear friend who has given me encouragement and support in *everything* I've tried to do during the past 15 years. I consider this person a "best friend" for several reasons and I am forever grateful.

Note to Reader

There is an 18-month span between the boys, and three years between my daughter and her first (older) brother.

My stories are 100 percent true—only the names have been omitted to prevent the kids from completely disowning me, although they all agreed the book needed to be written.

I apologized to my oldest that there weren't more references to him. He replied, *"That's ok—it means you only used my best stuff."*

I've started with my daughter and then moved on to her brothers. I have divided the book into ages 0-10 and 11-? Only by getting used to her personality will you appreciate the boys'. Have fun, and enjoy.

The stories and memories are meant to be cute, funny, and insightful. If you interpret them as anything else, you are taking your job (or mine) of parenting too seriously!

Family Portrait in 1989

Introduction

Since my daughter was born, I have told friends and coworkers of tales involving one, two, or all three of my kids. As they got older, the stories got funnier.

Friends who heard the stories encouraged me to write them down because "someday [I'd] be able to write a book." To all of them I say, "Voile!"

##

I've told a lot of stories over the past 18 years; these are some of the favorites that I've managed to remember. They'll no doubt put a smile on your face and perhaps allow you to remember stories about your own children that you should share with others.

I encourage readers to send me their own stories—maybe they'll be the basis for another book.

##

I'm pretty sure babies aren't born with a sense of humor, but I do believe that some children instinctively see the world differently than most. My three are among them; to each other, they've always made perfect sense.

They just marched to their own drummers (even when there wasn't a band). They aren't exceptional, but they *are* unique.

Is humor inherited? I doubt it. Can it be taught? Most definitely.

##

I believe humor is more an attitude than an art.

My father has entertained his children and grandchildren with stories of his youth, his family, our family, each other, and his ever-questionable military exploits.

The situations as he described them certainly follow the rest of the humor in the book and, quite honestly, are so funny I doubt he could have made them up.

He not only taught us to laugh at ourselves (and him), but also to view many circumstances in a positive (if not humorous) light. When we were growing up, many of our friends spent at least one evening with us and Dad, listening to stories while we laughed ourselves (and them), to tears.

Just when they thought we'd told all our stories, one of us would remember something else. If they had not fled in horror by the end of the evening, they were always welcome to return (and most did).

##

When I was five, my father helped me plant a garden in the backyard of our small, suburban home in a bedroom community with a population of about 22,000. Unlike other homes in the neighborhood with flowers in their gardens, my garden had corn.

According to Dad, I sat and watched for hours, waiting for the stalks to bloom or grow.

One day, he told me to put my bike away. Instead, I took it for a spin around the block before I returned it to the garage. As expected, after it was put away, I returned to the garden.

While I was gone, he'd *planted* a *can* of corn, making sure only a bit of the aluminum was shining through the dirt as the sunlight hit the rim. It was barely visible, but I noticed it right away! I dug it up, ran up and down the street shouting and showing everyone, and insisted that my mother cook the [creamed] corn for dinner.

##

Preface

Before my kids were born, I [thought] I wanted three blonde-haired, blue-eyed little girls who would sit quietly on the sofa in white pinafore dresses with patent leather shoes. Of course, I also imagined them doing needlepoint or embroidery all day.

Wow! Did that dream shatter quickly!

##

To begin with, the first two were boys. Before my daughter was born, our 15-year-old [male] babysitter commented on the decibel level in our house when the boys were playing and having a good time with him. So much for quiet, although the two youngest *were* blonde.

##

The children don't necessarily look like me, but they have two traits I am extremely proud to call my own—creativity and a sense of humor.

##

When my daughter was born, the boys were three and five. She was so active that I could hardly keep up with her, and so verbal that everything she said made me laugh.

##

When I saw how the boys responded to her, I started watching the dynamics between all of them, and found them to be very funny. This is when I realized that no matter how different these children are, they are all very much alike.

Not everything in this book requires an explanation, but I have tried to shed light in some situations. Details are included, where needed, to give insight into the personality of the children involved.

Four years ago, my daughter suggested I write a book about *"all the really silly stuff we say (and do)."* When I told her it was already in progress, she agreed to draw the pictures.

Now 18, she has already written and illustrated her first book which can be found online at www.stores.lulu.com/slwriter1120.

I DRAW STUFF

AGES 0-10

Once Upon A Time, There Was a Princess

AGES 0-1

You'll find that our interactions and conversations aren't what you'd expect from a child of her age; she has always been precocious.

Toward the end of my last pregnancy, the doctor decided on Friday to do an emergency C-section on Tuesday because the baby was positioned sideways and was no longer a candidate for natural delivery.

With an ultrasound scheduled, I insisted on knowing whether the baby was a boy or a girl. To my delight, the results indicated that in all likelihood I was having a girl, but I was cautioned that there was always a possibility it would be a boy.

That was close enough for me.

Her profile was completely visible through the blurred image. The quality of the film was not as good as they are today, where you can see "a real baby." Back then, what you saw was a lot of "snow" and a few dark spaces.

The technician would excitedly point to the image and declare parts to be a heart or a head.

She was as adorable the day before she was born as she is today (although she is a little bigger).

##

She has been a wonderful challenge from the minute she was delivered. It took her pediatrician 12 hours to get her breathing on her own.

We later learned that, because of the position at the time of birth, her hip sockets hadn't formed correctly.

She spent the first four months of her life bundled up in a little harness that kept her knees bent and strapped against her, to allow the joints of her hips an opportunity to form. She resembled a little parcel package, and we could only rest her in her swing, since her legs didn't dangle through the openings.

Little did I imagine that three years later I would be chasing her around the house, removing her from the tops of the kitchen and bathroom counters, the refrigerator, and the dryer, reminding her not to walk on the back of the couch or on the coffee table, and scolding her for other dangerous mischief she'd get into.

Baby in a Harness

##

She could tell the difference between whole milk, skimmed milk, 1 percent, 2 percent, etc. When her bottle was empty (or contained a *grade* of milk she didn't like), she'd heave it overhand from her crib with enough force to bounce off the farthest wall.

The first time, we laughed—then we made sure plastic bottles were always filled and on hand.

##

At 18 months, she locked herself into her grandpa's spare room and I needed help from his tenant to crawl through a window and rescue her!

We were trying to motion for her to turn the knob, and she just kept waving as if to say, "Hi." This all happened within the first two hours of our arrival.

The kind tenant asked me (with hesitation), *"How long will you be staying here?"*

##

When I combed her hair into pigtails, her brothers would call the style *"Bullwinkles"* (after the moose).

##

The babysitter often informed me, *"Her Majesty is in a mood today!"*

##

She would occasionally complain, *"No one told me I was beautiful today."*

##

I didn't condone her brothers' practice of drinking directly out of a community soda bottle, but there wasn't changing Dad, so we know where she learned this one. She would try to hold a two-liter bottle of soda (or worse, a gallon of milk), to her mouth and more than once ended up with a face full of whatever she was trying to drink.

##

AGES 2-3

We used to remark that we had found *"Rosemary's Baby"* because she could be a terror at times. As she got older and more mature, I would lovingly refer to her my "Devil Daughter."

My darling devil opened the refrigerator and deposited cracker crumbs into yet another two-liter bottle of soda. When her father came to the refrigerator for a swig, he took a long chug and immediately spit it out, asking (loudly), *"Who put this s*** in the soda?"*

She promptly corrected, *"Daddy, you're supposed to say poop."*

Several years later, I introduced her to a coworker as my *"Devil Daughter."*

The coworker replied, "*Oh, nonsense; I'm sure you're a lovely young woman.*"

My daughter replied, *"Oh, you haven't seen me at home!"*

##

At two, she created a huge wave across the waterbed. As I rolled over to see who was getting me up so early in the morning, she was at the side of the bed holding a gallon of milk (which she had hoisted and thumped onto the surface of the mattress) in one hand, and her bottle in the other.

Her demand was brief, but adamant: *"Fill it!"*

##

Six months later, she again woke me in the middle of the night to see *"the 'neat mess' [she] made."*

As she grabbed my hand and excitedly led the way upstairs to the kitchen to view her creation, I found 12 slimy egg whites and yokes—blended with shells—on the floor in front of the refrigerator.

She beamed proudly as she exclaimed, *"I wanted to see if they would all break!"*

##

By now she was *a lot* taller than other children her age. In addition to looking older, she could actually carry on an (albeit short) conversation.

When she was almost three, we visited the public library for a weekly playgroup. About halfway through the hour, she stood up, pointed down to a child sitting on the floor, looked up at his mother and asked, *"Is this your baby?"*

I cringed with embarrassment, as I explained that she and the *"baby" were* the same age.

When I took her to the grocery store, she would point to items on the shelf, naming them as we walked by. If there was something she didn't know, I'd tell her what it was; we had constant dialogue from the moment we entered the store.

An elderly man walked up behind me and whispered, *"You two make a wonderful team!"*

I thanked him and smiled—inside and out.

Around the ages of two and three, she wouldn't wear clothes unless she had personally picked them out and removed them from the drawers. But, she wouldn't wear shoes at all.

A neighbor gave her a pair of used, worn, red, high-top sneakers—she loved them! For the next year or

two, every outfit she wore had to include those sneakers.

##

They looked especially unique with long, ruffled "tea dresses." Not one to let frilly dresses slow her down, she loved wearing them to play outside. Her daycare provider asked me to send her in pants because the dresses kept getting tangled in the spokes of the tricycle.

##

A family with an adorable little boy moved next door. One day, I watched my daughter wander across the lawn and sit down in the dirt to play with him. They became instant friends. For weeks, I watched them through the window as they played next door or with toys in our yard.

One day while I was inside, I heard him calling from his yard, and thought he was hurt. I ran to look out the front door and realized he was calling my daughter to play. He was screaming, *"I need you!"*

She ran to an open window in the living room and hollered back, *"Ok, I just have to put my pants on!"*

Later that summer, I formally introduced myself to his mother. We both noticed how well they played together and I asked how old the young boy was.

His mother replied, *"Oh, he's much younger; he's only three."* Imagine her surprise when I laughed and said, *"So is she!"*

##

She loved to play in the puddle at the end of the driveway when it rained. She loved her little "pool"—it was almost two feet deep.

When neighbors drove by, they knew to slow down, look, and wave to see if she was splashing away.

Years later, neighbors would tell her, *"I used to wave at you when you splashed in the driveway."*

##

When she accompanied the boys and dad fishing on more than one occasion, I dressed her in overalls and sneakers.

Every time they returned, daddy would lift her by the straps and offer her back to me, dripping wet and covered with mud explaining, *"She fell in, again."*

##

<u>AGES 4-5</u>

While waiting for our order at a local pizza parlor, we were looking through pages of a magazine when she pointed to the models on a page and said, *"I call these 'beauties', but Al Bundy[1] calls them Hot Babes!"*

Of course, it sounded a lot louder to me than it probably was, but her point had been well made and I monitored her TV viewing habits more closely after that.

[1]reference to *Married with Children…* on *Fox TV*

##

Walking through the local mall with her grandpa and two brothers and me, she announced loudly, "I farted!"

Papa asked, "Who taught her that?" The boys answered, in unison, "We did!" It was obvious they were very proud of her.

##

On a trip to a grocery store, an older African-American gentleman slipped on something near us and let out a loud, *"Whoops!"* to which my daughter added, *"There it is!"* [2]

I was embarrassed and let out a nervous laugh, because clearly it wasn't the most politically-correct situation, but the reaction of the delighted shopper was perfect—he came over and gave her a "high five" and walked away repeating (just above a whisper), *"Whoops, there it is!"*

[2]reference to *"Whoomp! There It Is"* by Tag Team 1993

##

On her first day of nursery school, she was very excited. As I showed her the classroom, I told her there were two other children with the same first name (but spelled differently).

She looked at me puzzled and asked, *"Then how will I know who I am?"*

##

She said she needed a diary to write down all her *secret thoughts*. I thought it was cute, because she couldn't read *or* write yet, and I wasn't exactly sure what her secret thoughts might be. Yes, I bought her the diary.

##

Whenever I baked, I would set her up with supplies and a small cake mix, an egg, and some water; so she could "pretend" to make a cake.

It worked, because she would have fun and would keep busy for a while, but I'd laugh to myself when she'd sneeze into the bowl, or dump half an egg—complete with shell—into the mix. She'd end up covered in chocolate, and I'd march her directly into the tub as soon as our mixes were in the oven.

One day, while I was putting her cake in the oven, her brothers came to me with what they considered to be a very important concern. They had decided that we should serve *her* cake, too, so she wouldn't feel bad. *I* knew, however, that they just wanted more cake.

So, from then on, she baked for her brothers, because they were the only ones that would eat it until she was old enough to take minimal safety precautions.

##

She came to me and complained, *"I was watching the cat for hours, and when I went to pet her, I found out it was [her brother's] shoe!"*

When I took her to have her eyes examined for the first time, she wasn't old enough to read. The doctor assured me it would be fine because he used stencils and pictures she would recognize.

I heard later from the doctor that when he asked her what she saw, she said, *"It's a stupid picture of a stupid cake."*

##

Like the boys, she also had food allergies. I once took her to several specialists (pediatrician, ophthalmologist, allergist, etc.) in an effort to determine what was causing her eyes to swell and purple streaks to form down her face.

Her pediatrician thought she had an eye infection and prescribed drops, her ophthalmologist thought she was having a reaction to the drops and prescribed cream, the allergist said he had no idea.

By shear luck, I took her for an eye exam

and her optometrist recognized the problem immediately.

"Those are shiners," he said. *"They come from milk allergies."* Since I could think of nothing that had changed in her diet, we were stumped; until we stopped into the pizza parlor where we purchased dinner every Tuesday night and learned that they had just changed cheese vendors. So, not only did we learn about her allergy and worked to correct it, we also changed restaurants—which we have used for over 15 years now.

Finally learning to write, she would ask me to draw letters in the air—instead of writing them on a piece of paper—to see how they were formed.

##

She surprised me by making hand puppets one day. She couldn't read, but she understood what she saw.

She had cut out two mitten-shaped pieces of notebook paper and stapled them around the edges.

When I asked how she learned to do that, she took me to a pile of supplies (paper, scissors, stapler, and Brownie book she had found somewhere in the house), and pointed to the pictures illustrating Steps 1, 2, and 3.

##

She attended nursery school in the neighborhood, and shared a class with several local children. One child came from a Bolivian family and lived walking distance to our house.

From what I understood, there were several children—and grandparents—in their house, and the parents worked days. Spanish and English were spoken in the home, but the grandparents didn't speak English at all.

On days when she played there, she would come home eating an apple or a cookie, and tell me that "the Grandma" gave it to her. She suggested to me that "the Grandma" should learn English, so she could understand [my daughter] when she tried to speak to her.

I smiled and tried to explain that it would be easier for my daughter to learn Spanish than for "the Grandma" to learn English.

Sometime later that year, my daughter started reciting Spanish vocabulary words.

Silly me, I thought "the Grandma" was teaching her Spanish. I was thrilled as she recited: "*gato* means *cat, loco* means *crazy, agua* means *water, manzana* means *apple, mañana* means *tomorrow*," and on and on until the last phrase, when she said, "*And Speedy Gonzales is the fastest mouse in all of Mexico!*"

It was Looney Tunes[3], not "*the Grandma*," who was teaching her Spanish!

[3]reference Looney Tunes character Speedy Gonzales, first introduced in 1953

##

One day I took her with me to buy some bras and other items. I instructed her to look for a 3 and a __, and this many (insert number) D's.

She started looking, and I stepped back to see some items behind her. She stood up but didn't realize I was so close, so she shouted, *"I found a 3 and a __; how many D's do you need?"*

I blushed with embarrassment as everyone looked at me; but she had found the correct size.

We once found her sitting on top of the dryer, *"talking"* to a graham cracker.

I had taken her to the grocery store to buy dinner and she pointed at the mound of snack cakes the store had on display in the center of the back aisle.

She wanted all of them; I told her she couldn't have them because they were too expensive.

"That's ok," she said, "I *like* expensive things."

Nature was her playground, and there wasn't a pond or tree she wouldn't explore, a frog she wouldn't chase, or a beetle she wouldn't put in her mouth.

Now pets talked to her, and interestingly, she talks back to them.

The scary thing is that th*ey seem to understand her.*

Her kindergarten was a program integrated with special needs children; there were a few spots opened for children who were not yet tested for potential disabilities, she being one.

I had concerns that she was showing signs of Attention Deficit Disorder (ADD). Her pediatrician had refused to test her earlier, because *"[they] really don't get involved, unless discipline becomes a problem and parents are at their wits end."*

Bingo, I was there.

After consulting with her kindergarten teachers, I requested that she be tested which, I came to realize, included surveys, classroom monitoring, and generalized recommendations.

At her final consultation—where she was formally diagnosed —I entered the psychiatrist's office, sat down as instructed, and glanced at his desktop.

There were several reports within eyesight with the word "Severe" stamped on them. The doctor's first words to me were, *"Mrs. Williams, she's a doozy."*

It turns out she could have been a poster child for Attention Deficit Hyperactivity Disorder (ADHD). She was prescribed medication, but I was warned

that some children react favorably, and others don't. If she was going to respond, we would see a reaction almost instantly.

Within five hours of her first dose, we had a brand new five year-old. I waited a week before calling the doctor with a progress report because I didn't want to "jinx" my good luck.

Her father summed up the situation correctly when he suggested that the "bad baby fairy" had come and taken our "bad baby" away. She was never really bad, but she was a handful. The fairy had replaced her with a good baby.

Before medication, test results indicated a second grade verbal and academic level; after medication, she scored higher.

##

I was delighted to see that one of her take home papers had the American Sign Language alphabet on the back, with instructions how to practice at home. I thought it was wonderful that she was learning this skill. As I read the paper and looked at the practice exercises, I asked, *"Is there a child in your class that can't hear when you talk to them?"*

She put her hand on her hip, tilted her head, and said (loudly), *"Mom, everyone can hear me when I talk!"* The teacher later explained that she was expecting a deaf child during the middle of the school year, and she wanted the other children able to communicate with him by the time he arrived.

AGES 5-6

I took her and the boys out for ice cream at a local stand on her birthday, and for whatever reason, she said to the clerk, "Today's my birthday—do I get mine for free?"

I was shocked—and scolded her while we were waiting for her cone. The woman (who turned out to be an owner) said to me, "Don't worry—if she's bold enough to ask for it, she's entitled to it."

Sports took on a completely new dimension when she was involved. One cannot fully appreciate 18 holes of miniature golf if you haven't played it with a hyperactive child. Two adults and three kids flew through the course in a record-setting 25 minutes!

She was definitely a tomboy, so I had to explain that she couldn't wear her favorite pink velvet dress (from Grandma) to T-ball[4] practice.

[4] reference T-ball is pre-baseball for 4-6 years olds

##

AGE 7

One day, when we were helping to coach her basketball team, she decided to leave the court in the middle of practice. With her arms outstretched, she let the ball fall away and ran across the court to say, "Huggies!"

I guess you're never too young or too old to need a hug.

She overheard her father and me discussing boring movies. She put her hand on her hip and said, *"If you want to see a really boring movie, see 'Free Willey 2'."*

When we asked if she had seen it, she rolled her eyes, hand still on her hip, and replied, *"No, but trust me, it's boring!"*

On her seventh birthday, she complained to her father that he hadn't given her any birthday presents yet.

He looked at me, as though I had somehow forgotten to give her gifts at her huge party. No, she explained, she wanted *special* birthday presents (like the ones her brothers got).

She told her Dad, *"I want a ride on your motorcycle and I want to shoot a .22."*

He said she did better than the boys on their first visits to the range.

##

When the microwave broke, she thought she'd never have popcorn again

##

She asked for an Easy Bake Oven because the microwave wasn't fast enough!

##

We caught her hugging the microwave and proclaiming, *"I am the Queen, and this is my Food Kingdom!"*

##

I watched as she manipulated the joystick of a pinball game located just past the checkout aisle of a local department store. She could barely see over the base of the machine, and definitely couldn't see the play screen, but she enjoyed *pretending* to play.

A teenage boy came over to the machine and stood by her for a few minutes, watching her "play."

Then he deposited quarters into the machine and appeared to politely ask her to move aside. She moved, but stayed, watching.

When my purchases were paid for, I called her to join me as I was leaving the store. I was amazed when the teen turned to me and said, *"Please Lady, let her stay; she's winning!"*

He had put an extra quarter in so she could play against him.

##

Disney re-released a movie in 1996, and she pleaded for me to take her to see *101 Damnations.*

Likewise, she kept telling me her friend from school lived in a compartment [apartment].

##

With an Older Brother

AGES 0-1

My youngest son was ten pounds when he was born, and even though he was a wonderful baby, he cried *a lot*.

I couldn't help but wonder if he was hungry, even though he nursed at least every two hours.

Everyone at the doctor's office asked me not to give him solids until he was at least six months old, but by four months, I was listening to mothers who suggested introducing something sweet into his diet, like carrots or blueberries.

They felt the sweetness might encourage him to try the food if he was resistant, and that just a taste might satisfy him.

Cautiously, I put a bit of carrots on the smallest spoon I had, and placed it to his lips. He loved it! His eyes opened wide, his hands and feet started flailing, and he seemed genuinely happy. I gave him a full spoonful, and he was thrilled.

His first "taste" of baby food ended up being two-and-a-half *jars*. From then on, he slept through the night as long as he had a few jars of food during the day.

##

I joined a "Mommy and Me" program at our local YWCA when he was eight weeks old, but found myself telling other mothers that he was *four months* old because he was so big. He was already wearing a [size 9 months] grey sweat suit.

After enrolling him in infant care at 10 months old, an item on the list of daily requirements was baby food. It took a few weeks to convince the teacher that I he ate two peanut butter and jelly sandwiches torn into little pieces on his highchair tray.

Today he's over 6 feet tall and thin as a rail.

##

AGES 1-2

At two, his teacher told me he refused to finger-paint with pudding. No problem, I answered, *"Give him a paintbrush."* He didn't like dirty hands!

##

His favorite color (or word) was yellow, but he pronounced it "Lello;" and *everything* was "Lellow."

##

Starting about the time he was old enough to walk, he insisted on picking out his own clothes, and wearing colors like neon green, purple and orange together, so I went out and bought him a few pairs of rainbow-colored, striped suspenders —and added them to every outfit.

##

When he was old enough to understand, I took him to the grocery store to see the frozen turkeys. I'd point to one that was 10 pounds and tell him, *"That's how big you were when you were born!"*

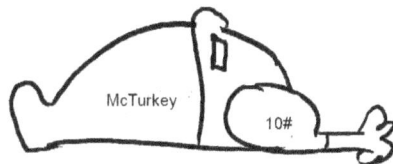

##

AGE 3

We celebrated his third birthday with their grandmother on the same day we celebrated my daughter's first birthday. After we had provided her with a whole cake and a balloon, and let her have her fill, my mother took something off the top of the refrigerator, decorated in birthday wrapping, and said to my son, "And look what I have up here for you!"

For weeks prior to this visit, my son had been asking for a toy that I knew grandma was going to get him for his birthday. After his incessant whining, I told him, "I think Grandma is going to get it for you, but don't let her know I told you."

Well, when Grandma put the package in front of him, (but before he had opened it), he said, "Oh Grandma! It's just what I've always wanted!" At which point I had to suggest he *open* the gift and thank her again.

##

One of my favorite memories of my cherubic blonde-haired, blue-eyed, child who stared in amazement from the back of a shopping cart at the lobsters in the tank at
the grocery store.

He pointed and hollered,
"Look at the humongous bugs!"

##

When we told him I was pregnant and would be having another baby, he told me, "We don't _need_ another baby—_I'm_ your baby!"

##

Later during the pregnancy, he pointed at my very round belly and said, _"You've got a basketball in there!"_

##

After a particularly hard day, I threatened to throw out all his toys if he didn't pick them up off the floor of his room.

Ten or fifteen minutes later, he came into the kitchen with his arms full of toys and said, _"You can throw them all out, because I'm not going to pick them up!"_

##

His nursery school teacher called me in for a conference because she was concerned that he "_spoke in paragraphs_," and the other children spoke in three-and-four-word sentences.

The teachers were uncomfortable because he "_couldn't communicate with the other children._"

So, I enrolled him in a different school, around the corner from our home.

##

AGES 4-5

He walked in on me as I stepped out of the shower one day and said, *"Mommy! You look so much prettier with all your clothes on!"*

##

During a well-child visit, his pediatrician reminded me, *"Remember, no peanuts for children this age."* He continued, *"The rule is, kids can't eat it till they can spell it."*

My son replied, *"P.E.A.N.U.T.S.—now can I have them?"* What else could the doctor do?

He said, *"Well, I suppose you can!"*

##

When his older brother was six, we bought a popular video game system to help his [brother's] fine and gross motor coordination.

A little concerned that he would want to play, I asked the doctor; he assured us that a four-year-old didn't have the attention span or the coordination to play video games, so we really didn't consider that he might try.

One day, he started to walk passed the game, and picked up the controller.

He figured out how to turn the system on, and proceeded to score 100,000 points.

His father and I stared in amazement as he played! We were never able to match that score, no matter how many hot summer nights we spent playing late into the evening or early into the morning.

We deduced that four-year-olds must think magic mushrooms and flying turtles *are* around every corner.

##

The children and I came home from dinner at a pizza parlor when he handed me a salt shaker from the restaurant. I was shocked, and asked why he took it.

He pointed to the word *Steel* (as in stainless) and thought it was an invitation to *steal.* We promptly returned it to the restaurant.

##

A month prior to starting kindergarten, he asked me, "How come I can't put my thumb all the way up?" When I asked him what he meant, he showed me that his thumb was cocked at a slight angle, and that he couldn't straighten it.

I remember thinking I must be terribly negligent that I had never noticed this, but he told me that he hadn't shown me because he thought I would be mad?

Needless to say, it was taken care of quickly. The doctor's had to do surgery on the muscle to release what they termed a "trigger finger." Thanks to surgery, he missed his first day of kindergarten.

He was put in charge of installing programs into the computer at his kindergarten class—he even earned a math award when he graduated.

We joined my in-laws each Christmas, but didn't celebrate at home. I explained that the man named Santa who came to Grandma's house to leave presents for their cousins was really their Grandpa *pretending* to be Santa.

We made a pledge to play along, and to keep the secret. I didn't think too much of it when my friend asked to take my kids to see Santa in the local shopping mall. She waited in line for her children (and mine) to sit on Santa's lap.

When she dropped them home, she asked me why my son had asked Santa, *"Whose Grandpa are you?"*

##

AGE 8

His best quote ever, "I could handle pain, if it didn't hurt!"

From the first day of elementary school, he skated through the grades with little or no effort. In first grade, we had to convince his teacher to provide extra work, as he was testing far in advance of his classmates.

##

Her first response was that he had to learn to wait until the rest of the class caught up to him. We knew that wasn't going to happen anytime soon, so we asked her to give him extra work at night so that he would have something to do that would keep him interested and discourage boredom. We were afraid that if he was constantly bored, he'd eventually become disruptive.

##

The math problems she sent home (under the condition that we kept the arrangement confidential) were still far below his capability, so one night, his father decided to send a quadratic equation back to her.

Yes, it was far in advance of his ability, but it woke her up regarding the individual nature of our requests to accommodate him.

Example of a quadratic equation: $x^2 + 2x = 8$

##

In future grades, he got by without doing homework or completing required assignments. I even tried to reason with him that he couldn't keep getting 40's on his spelling tests, because his mom was a writer. So, on the next test, he got a 50.

##

He was also very content to "just get by." No matter how poorly he performed, he received wonderful progress reports and report cards. When I asked his teachers "why," in almost every grade, I was told, "because we know he can do the work."

I tried to protest and even requested that he even be kept back if he did not perform, I was told that it was almost unheard of to keep a child (who was capable of doing the required work) behind.

##

When he and his sister were five and eight, they came to me with a plan to open the *"All We Can Do"* Beauty Salon.

Their gimmick? They were going to bring people in and give them terrible haircuts and, when the customers complained, tell them, *"Sorry, that's all we can do!"*

##

<u>AGE 9</u>

He entered an essay contest with a very short entry and, as the teacher instructed, used spell check.

However, he managed to select every *wrong* spelling choice possible, resulting in a charmingly poor example of an essay, but one I kept hanging over my desk for a long time.

So much for not insisting that students know how to spell.

We hoped he'd become as involved in Scouting as his brother was, but it just wasn't going to happen. After his first camping trip, he returned home complaining, *"They don't just let you go camping—they make you <u>do</u> stuff."*

He gave winter camping a try (at the encouragement of his brother) but, when he got home, he was walking stiff as a board. He told us, *"Don't ever let me do that again!"*

Against my wishes, he stopped scouting, accusing me of *"ruining his life"* (for not wanting him to quit).

##

<u>AGE 10</u>

In fourth grade, he started handing me papers to sign every morning before he left for school (i.e. not having homework turned in, not being organized, etc.). Once again, I thought it was a situation of "we know he can do it."

Because I knew he *wasn't* organized, had a habit of *not* doing homework, and/or doing homework and *not turning it in*, I wasn't terribly surprised, but I was concerned. As the year went on, the papers kept coming at least once or twice a week.

His progress reports looked fine, but I couldn't understand why I was still signing notes. I was also a little upset that I hadn't heard from his teacher at all, considering the number of papers I was being handed.

I finally took matters into my own hands (I thought) and started by asking my son what it would take to motivate him to pass, since I was afraid all the signed notes were going to hinder his advancement to fifth grade, despite the "no student left behind" philosophy.

I should have known better when he asked if he could pierce his ear if he passed. In a moment of weakness, I agreed.

Next, I made an appointment with his teacher, who was more than happy to meet with me. He did, however, seem completely unaware of the

reason for my visit.

I stated my concerns, and asked for an explanation about the papers I had been signing. I asked why he hadn't contacted me with what appeared (to me) to be quite a problem.

He looked at me in amazement and a sly smile formed across his face. He leaned back in his chair and politely handed his grade book for me to examine.

As I reached for it, I mentioned the bargain we had made about piercing his ear. Now, he leaned all the way back in his chair, arms folded above his head, legs crossed with feet on the desk, and laughed. *"Suretta,"* he said, *"You've been had!"*

Apparently, my son had gotten hold of a stack of form letters (i.e. disciplinary notes) that the teacher kept on a shelf. Since all that was required was an X in the proper box, my son had filled in the X's and brought them to me, one at a time.

His teacher knew nothing of the notes, because they were never turned in (although he said that he *had* wondered where they'd all gone), and my son was carrying an A+ in the class.

Not only that, he had been bragging to the class that he was going to get his ear pierced. Yes—fourth grade pictures clearly show an earring in one ear, which was a phase that lasted less than a year when he learned he had to remove it to play baseball.

As I watched him play first base on our town's 10-year-old All-Star team, I was a bit unhappy with the way our team was being represented.

I asked if these weren't the best players, and I was corrected by his father, *"they're not the best; they're just the best we have."* Enough said.

##

I also watched with amusement as he entertained himself by dancing on base, since none of the balls were being directed to him and he was getting bored.

He played well; and was able to catch a ball quite a distance from the plate without moving at least one foot. There were teammates that asked him, *"don't you have any bones?"* commenting on his flexibility.

##

At another game, he ran toward the base and collided face first with the catcher's kneepads. His nose was bleeding profusely, and teammates and coaches stopped to assist the "wounded soldier."

##

I waited a few minutes before starting to walk out to the field, and I was walking out as other players were telling me how badly he was hurt. When I saw the coaches prop him up and guide him back to position, I retreated back to the stands.

Other mothers asked why they were making him finish out the game (as if I knew).

Later, the coaches told me that he *begged* to go back out onto the field—and as long as he wanted to play, they were going to let him.

Interesting Accidents

He was terribly accident prone and managed to hurt himself in almost every endeavor he undertook.

##

When he was three, I came home to find his father attending to a gaping wound on his forehead. When I asked what happened, he [my son] told me that his brother hit him in the head with a shovel.

When I questioned his brother, he confirmed, "I hit him in the head with a shovel." At least they don't lie, I guess.

##

He jammed his thumb knuckle playing basketball at a friend's house, resulting in a trip to the emergency room and a large gauze bandage. As we left the ER, he asked, "Can I still play baseball?"

##

He was riding his bike down the road when he plowed into a neighbor's wooden mailbox post and severed it where the box is fastened to the post.

##

When he was a little bit older, he was skateboarding and landed on the edge of a concrete foundation, leaving a huge bump on his shin. It was the first time he had ever called for a ride home—from almost anywhere.

##

He went snowboarding for the first time in junior high, fell and managed to scrape the entire side of his face *and* lose a molar in the process.

##

Although he quit Boy Scouts, he enjoyed accompanying his sister's Brownie troop on their bowling expeditions when he was ten. He didn't even mind being dubbed him an *"Honorary Brownie."*

##

At his grandparents' house on Christmas Day, listening to grownups talk and argue about politics or something of equal disinterest to children, he commented, *"Mom—Dad sure gets mad when he doesn't know what he's talking about!"*

He found a large stash of change on his father's dresser, took the change, then took the money to his father and asked if he'd give him dollars for the change.

Dad would take the change, give him dollars, and put the change back on his dresser. It took Dad a few times to realize his son was draining the same dish with the same money and profiting again and again.

He was a tough one when it came to money. We offered him an allowance of a dollar for different weekly chores; and "counter offered" that he wanted a dollar for each drawer he opened. Of course, we out-voted his request.

One night after he lost a tooth, I noticed that he hadn't removed the dollar from under his pillow, so I took it back. I figured he could use the same tooth and I'd keep putting the same dollar back again. He must have overheard me telling his father, because later I heard him telling a friend that he was going to keep putting the same tooth under his pillow until he saved up $299.

##

And They Had a Bigger Brother
<u>AGES 0-1</u>

We had a tough time with the oldest—now 23. He never crawled—he rolled. He never slept—he cried. If he fell asleep being held, he'd wake up when we put him down. He'd cry when we left the room, and didn't have an eating or sleeping pattern.

By 13-months, he routinely got out of his crib. In order to childproof the house, we put sliding locks at the tops of doors, instead of obstructing the handles or adding plastic latches.

Six years later, when my daughter was two, she figured how to use the end of the broom handle to slide the locks open.

At his baby shower, I had received a musical clown. I thought it was adorable, but never knew the impact it would have on our life. When he was crying one day, I wound up the clown and sat it next to him.

He reached for it and it became a constant companion—especially at bedtime. If he couldn't find his clown, he wasn't going to sleep.

The clown was so important that after we returned home from a visit to the grandparents, his father turned the car right around (after dropping us off) and drove back another hour,

because we had inadvertently left the clown behind.

We had also bought a musical attachment that went between the gap on the crib. It was arc shaped, and a "happy cloud" would slide up and down the arch.

The little tune was annoying, but it helped put him to sleep, so we rewound it several times before we could stop it.

Soon after we got it, there was an ad campaign on TV for of the item. Every time the ad came on, we jumped up and made sure the music wasn't coming from the nursery. We were beginning to hear the tune in our sleep.

A beautiful long-haired orange cat had found his way to our home. We took her in and adopted hiim, just prior to my son's birth. When he was as young as three months old, we would prop him up on the couch.

The cat would park herself in his lap, keeping him upright. When he started to tip, if we didn't catch him first, he'd grab hold of her fur to steady himself. For the entire time he slept in a crib, the cat slept underneath. She was his constant companion and bodyguard, and I even caught him trying to eat dry cat food from her dish.

When I consulted his pediatrician, I was told it was probably one of the healthiest things a baby could put in their mouths.

Needless to say, it only happened once.

<u>AGES 1-2</u>

He was three feet tall, and looked like he was four or five. People would talk to him and then wonder why he didn't answer. I would have to explain that he was only 18 months old.

His first words (garbled as they were), spoken after his teacher vowed he'd talk by the time he was two (he was a year younger than everyone else in his class) were, "*I Did It!*"

On his college graduation cake, we wrote "*You Did It!*"

##

AGES 3-4

In his nursery school picture, he is posed leaning against a tree. Who knew that 15 years later he'd be earning state recognition awards for Tree Identification or, a few years later, be Nature Director at Boy Scout Camp?

##

When he was a little older, he would point to things and grunt or whine. Finally, one day, when he was about three, he was pointing at the cupboard and grunting.

Exasperated, I said, *"Why don't you just get what you're pointing at?"*

From nowhere he answered, *"But Mommy, I can't reach it."*

I don't think anyone else would have understood him, but I sure did.

##

He was so proud the day he learned his name. *"I know my name, I know my name!"* he repeated excitedly, until I said, *"Ok, what's your name?"*

He answered, very proudly, *"Bobby[5] Green!"* But, Bobby Green was the *other* Bobby in class!

[5]Bobby is a fictitious name

##

He didn't talk much until he was five, but at some point in nursery school, he came home from school saying, *"Ho, Ho."*

We had no idea what he was trying to tell us.

He couldn't explain himself; he could just repeat *"Ho, Ho."*

Friends suggested he might want the cookies that were similar to Oreos™, but they weren't the same; I tried treats like Ring Dings™, but he continued to walk around saying, *"Ho-Ho,"* as though he wanted something.

We finally gave up in desperation and he eventually stopped asking but, sure enough, his younger brother started the same thing at a different school. I couldn't help wondering what the schools were giving (or teaching) the children that made them long for *"Ho Ho."*

Again, I asked people at the school if they had any idea what he was talking about and I got pretty much the same answers I did a few years ago, with the oldest.

Three years later, when my daughter was two or three, she started saying, *"Ho, Ho,"* but she wasn't in nursery school at all! I asked her what she meant when she said that, she answered, *"Santa says Ho, Ho!"*

##

His birthday is in the middle of the summer, so we had large outdoor parties. On his fourth birthday, I planned a "Double Dare" theme (after the Nickelodeon Show).

I invited everyone from his class and asked parents to send bathing suits and a change of clothes. My intention was to hose all the children off outdoors, dry them off, and then send them inside to change.

Most of the parents were familiar with the television show and knew that a mess was the ultimate result—"slime" was just becoming popular.

One of the parents was "older" than most of us—if we were in our 20's, I would guess him to be at least 50. We don't know if he was a stepfather or just a "new" parent, but he seemed puzzled when he opened the invitation at school.

It was obvious he wasn't familiar with the TV program, and he asked if he could stay at the party to "watch" the fun.

By the end of the day, he was having more fun than his adorable daughter. We even put gumballs in the bottom of paper bowls and filled them with whipped cream. Without using their hands, the children had to eat the whipped cream down to the gumball. The hit of the party was a plastic slide that we had covered in chocolate sauce and whipped cream. We kept it until the end, and the kids had a blast. We let them all slide down once, and on the second turn, we turned on the hose and let them go down as many times as it took to clean them off.

Guess who was holding the hose? Yup, our new friend—the father!

By the time he was four, my son suffered from several health conditions including migraines, sinus infections, behavioral problems, learning disabilities, etc.

After reading a book by a noted physician, I started testing him for food allergies. I already knew he was lactose intolerant, but it was soon apparent that he was allergic to red dye. I had removed hot dogs, nitrates, sugar, peanuts, and other possible sources of trouble. In fact, the boys had morning cereal with orange juice fortified with calcium rather than milk for the first five years of their lives.

Soon after, we noticed that he would be sick as soon as his course of medicine was through so, every 10 days, he was back at the doctor's office. A new doctor put him on a white medicine instead of the usual pink-based medicine and the symptoms cleared up right away.

While his doctor's claimed it wasn't possible, I also found he reacted negatively to pink laundry detergent and body soap. He was also very sensitive and I had to use fragrance-free products.

I didn't know which was harder—convincing his doctors that

he reacted to red dye, or teaching a four-year-old the difference between foods that were naturally red (like strawberries) and those with red dye (like popsicles).

Because of his several problems, I was very careful about what the boys ate—with very little refined sugar in their diet.

One day, when they came home from school, they were trying to describe something a classmate was eating at school. Once I was able to determine it was yellow, long, and had cream inside, I realized they were describing a Hostess Twinkie™!

At some later point in time, I brought home a treat of chocolate éclairs which, of course, the boys had never seen or eaten. For years, they continued to ask me to purchase "chocolate hotdogs" until they had outgrown the urge for pudding and chocolate in a hot-dog-like bun.

##

AGES 5-6

He came home from kindergarten one day and started asking for an earring. I couldn't imagine how or why he would want one, so I asked his teacher.

She mentioned that one of the boys had an earring because his father did—and that many of the children in the classroom looked up to him as though he "hung the moon."

Apparently, so did the mothers. The teacher suggested I show up a bit early someday—she said I'd recognize him immediately because he wore orange sneakers.

Around here, children (at least mine) are taught to equate a person's identity by something that does not distinguish race or other minority status. Thus, the teacher referring to an article of clothes, rather than, "The gorgeous Hispanic father," was something I was quite used to.

Orange sneakers and an earring were all I had to go on. I showed up about a half-hour early one day, and there were at least six mothers picking up their children, but the children seemed to be ready to go while the mothers stood chatting.

When "orange sneakers" walked in, every mother swooned— as a perfect specimen (and a relatively rare sight in this area) of a Hispanic young man entered the room.

Sure enough, he gathered up his son (who also had an earring), waved goodbye to the ladies, and left. Ok, I was sold. I told his father he wanted an earring.

After our initial conversation, a friend of mine explained (to me) that it was an old sailors' custom to wear an earring in one ear after he crossed the equator. The other ear was pierced on his return voyage. Pleading my son's case, I explained the tale to his father (I didn't mention "orange sneakers.")

His father answered, *"Fine, when he crosses the equator, he can have an earring."*

##

The son insisted he needed glasses. We had his eyes tested, and they were fine, but he insisted, so at the doctor's suggestion, we purchased a pair with clear lenses.

The optometrist suggested he might like a girl in his class who was wearing glasses. I doubted that, because the girl he had liked since age two didn't wear glasses, but there was clearly some desperate need he was voicing.

Sometime after that, we learned that he was suffering from ocular migraines, which cause visual distortions that he couldn't yet explain to us.

##

<u>AGE 9</u>

I was watching a documentary on alleged UFO sightings throughout the previous decades. He joined me as we heard interviews from people who claimed to have seen aliens, been abducted, or otherwise been prodded and probed by something.

When the program was over, he asked if the stories we had just seen were true. I explained that, to the people telling them, they were very real; however, not everyone believed them.

He waited a minute and then said, very thoughtfully, *"I don't think the stories are real."*

When I asked why, he said, *"Because you can't fit 12 Martians in a spaceship—you can only fit four or five."*

##

He came home from school with an assignment to write a letter to an important person, and there were certain elements that had to be included.

I believe the letter had to talk about a certain product, mention how the student liked or disliked it, and make a suggestion for a new way to use it.

As a creative writer, I thought this assignment was wonderful. I sat with my son as we decided to write to a toy manufacturer that made an electronic product that both my son and [then] husband enjoyed.

Together we researched on the Internet and found the real name and corporate address of the company's president.

In his letter, he explained the assignment and mentioned how his father played with the toy when he was an adult, and now [my son] was enjoying it, too.

He wrote of the reasons he liked it, and how he and his younger brother had constructed a flashlight (with no instructions) from the kit to assist me during a recent power outage.

Not being one to start a project and not finish it, I made a copy of the letter and actually mailed it, before my son passed in his assignment.

Within weeks, he received a personal response! He thanked him for his letter and spoke of how wonderful it was that father and son(s) could share the excitement of using the product.

He was also thanked for his suggestion of making a flashlight with the product and was assured it would be considered as something to be added in future versions.

I don't remember whether or not we gave the response to his teacher, but he was certainly the only letter that received a response.

##

AGES 11-?

Then They Grow Up

I had never taken her to buy school clothes before, so when she was 11, I agreed to let her shop with me. As we left for the store she asked, *"Will they weigh me when we're done shopping?"*

I was puzzled, to say the least, until I realized she had seen an episode of the Antiques Roadshow (which I watched regularly) and saw the conversion of British pounds to equivalent dollars.

She assumed they were weighing the item and then calculating its cost per pound.

##

On my daughter's 11th birthday, she attended an orientation evening for the Sea Cadets at the local Armed Forces Recruiting Station.

We were there for three hours and she attended a class with older teens, but ultimately decided that she wasn't interested in joining the Navy yet.

She did, however, sing, *"In the Navy"* on the way home, and asked if she could now march in a Veterans Day parade.

##

When she was 12, we went away overnight and left her in the care of her brothers. When I called to check in, she said, *"I colored my hair red—it came out just the way I wanted!"*

This wasn't a total shock, as we had discussed the possibility of using a *temporary* hair color solution, but I had not actually done any research on brands, colors, or the definition of *temporary.*

In addition, I was somewhat dreading her hair becoming candy-apple or fire engine red, although the resulting *auburn* color was absolutely beautiful.

It was her next statement that threw me: *"Now, Instead of people calling me a 'dumb blonde', they'll just think I'm stupid."*

I couldn't help but laugh and tell her, "That's the stupidest thing I've ever heard (and that she's ever said)."

For weeks later, she was experimenting with color. Because she hadn't bleached her hair first (thank goodness), the colors came out differently than shown on the boxes—and she kept trying. At one point I had to tell her to "pick a color and stick with

it," because the part in her hair had turned a lovely shade of purple.

##

For several years, she was fascinated with dragons—she particularly loved to draw them. When she was 12 or 13, she asked if I could find her a book on their lives. She wanted to know when they were born, where they lived, and what they looked like when they were little. I asked if she was looking for something on Greek or Oriental mythology, and she said, *"No."* I realized then that she thought they were real.

She's always had a very special bond with both brothers, but she's keenly connected to the younger of the two.

I once asked her if she had ever wished she had an older sister and she told me, *"I don't need a sister, I have [him]. He's stupid like an older brother but, yeah, he's a sister!"*

In anticipation of her first airplane ride at 12, she asked, *"What if I look out the window and see a bear on the wing?"*[6]

[6]*reference The Twighlight Zone, Terror at 20,000 Feet (1963)*

A while into the flight, after watching intently out the window, she asked why she couldn't see the outlines around the states (as if they were on a map).

As she read the instructions for emergency landings and how to slide through the escape chute to safety on the ground, she asked, *"When we get to the bottom, can we climb back up and do it again?"*

##

She had a bad cold and felt terrible, so I suggested she make a cup of hot tea.

Later she told me she had made the tea, and then put in a packet of *"whatever [I] use to make the tea taste better."*

I drink a lot of tea, but all I've ever put in was artificial sweetener. When I asked her to show me what she used to make it taste better, she showed me the box of teabags!

##

Before her 15th birthday, I heard an announcement that one of her favorite comedians was coming to a nearby town.

I was away on business, so I waited 20 minutes on hold (long distance) to secure four tickets to the show—six months in advance.

We invited her closest friend and treated them to a weekend away, complete with souvenir CDs, a night at a hotel with a pool, and other luxuries.

They laughed and enjoyed as the opening comedian came on stage, but there was still an element of anticipation. Once the headliner came out, we all enjoyed the show. They were thrilled to stand in line for an autograph and a handshake before we left.

As we waited, I suggested that daughter ask him to sign "Happy Birthday," but she was embarrassed. Her friend, however, asked me, *"Can I ask him to sign, 'Dear E-Bay*

Winner'?"

##

Halloween in our town is more social than anything else. Kids want candy, adults want candy, and neighbors have a good excuse to visit.

##

My daughter has been reading medical books for as long as I can remember. In fact, since fourth grade, most of the time she informs me of a problem or concern only after she has fully investigated and/or diagnosed herself; she has a pretty good track record.

##

Apparently, in health class during her junior year of high school, she became quite well known for answering or debating many of the subjects discussed in class. We've had several great discussions and she knows if she asks any questions on any topic, I'll give her a straight answer.

The problem is, she doesn't exactly understand 100 percent of the time, and many times, she takes things far too literally.

So, I was not entirely surprised to learn that she had told the class, *"If you want to know about heroin, you can talk to my mom—she works in a meth lab."*

Later I corrected her (and asked her to clarify to the class) that I worked in a *methadone clinic that treats heroin addicts.*

##

My daughter and the close same friend were trying to design Halloween costumes when the friend suggested they dress all in blue and attach cotton balls to themselves. They could carry squirt guns and go as *partly-cloudy-with-chance-of-rain-[wo] men!*

During her junior year of high school, I came home to find her close to tears because someone at school had nominated her for a leadership award.

To my understanding, this was an essay contest and the winner(s) won a week at a New York female leadership retreat.

When I asked why she was so upset, she explained that she didn't want to go to New York, but most importantly, she did not like with the nomination and entrant requirements.

She was to write an essay about something she felt strongly about, and how she would bring this subject to the forefront of the general public. She went on to say that not only did she not think a "white girl from New Hampshire," would actually *win* the contest, but there were questions that each entrant was required to fill out "in order to ensure diversity."

She ranted and raved for several hours about how she shouldn't have to provide information that employers and others had no legal right to ask, and was concerned because she had never been able to speak to or for others. In fact, she couldn't think of a single subject she was passionate about.

When it appeared she was through with her tirade, I suggested she write the essay about the requirements of this particular award. Her immediate reply was, *"Oh, I love irony."*

She even received a positive response from her guidance counselor about actually writing such a paper, but in the end, she didn't send in an essay.

##

Youngest Brother

When he was about 11, he wanted to come with me to a local thrift store. I stressed that he must behave. He was not to take anything off the shelf, play with the toys, run around, or become a nuisance.

In fact, my kids remember the "3 B" rules I established before we went into a store: *Be Good, Be Quiet, and B-have!*

##

So, he came into the store with me and had, up to then, behaved. I turned to pay at the register and was handing the woman money when we both heard a weak whine calling, *"Mom! Help!"*

I turned around to see that he had tried on a fur coat—but had not taken it off the hanger, which was locked to the rack.

Basically, he was stuck. I was mad, but started laughing until tears came from my eyes. As we left the store, I was still laughing and scolding him—he never did it again, but we'll always remember it.

##

He wanted a pocketknife and had asked before, but I had refused. His older brother had received certifications for carrying and using several knives in Scouting.

He was 11 now, so I agreed to *consider* allowing him to own one.

He told me he had seen the exact knife he wanted at the local flea market, so I took him to look at it the following week.

When we reached the display case, I saw a notice prominently displayed that read:

NO SALES TO MINORS WITHOUT A PARENT PRESENT

"Good sign," I thought.

My eyes glanced at the small display of pocketknives, and then immediately focused on the daggers and elaborate swords.

He showed me the pocketknife he wanted—it had an elaborate handle with a curved blade, and large serrated points that looked very, very sharp.

This was obviously not a pocketknife. This knife was clearly not sanctioned by the Boy Scouts of America.

He whined that he wanted it, carried on incessantly, and as a last ditch argument countered with, *"I can buy one because I have a parent with me."*

The vendor laughed, and promised not to sell this weapon to my son. We both explained to him that "without a parent present" did not mean he just had to have a parent with him, but his parent must also approve of the purchase.

I had visions of medieval weaponry (like big iron balls with spikes on them) hanging on his bedroom wall. Those would certainly add a new level to sibling rivalry—an advantage in any quarrel.

When he was about 14, I had forgotten to tell him that my daughter had a friend staying over—it was obvious he was not talking about his sister when he came to me and said, *"I knocked on [his sister's] door, and a little girl popped out."*

At 15, he had a good job at a reliable place that eventually hired him back for three consecutive summers.

I came home one afternoon to find him making lunch. When I asked why he was home so early, he told me he left because his boss was sleeping.

I instructed him to return—quickly!

An avid angler, he won a local fishing tournament, only to have someone steal his trophy before he claimed it.

##

After his first airplane flight at 15, he told me he'd join the Air Force Academy if he didn't have to fly in a plane to get there.

##

When his brother was picking out courses for one of his high school semesters, we were reviewing the requirements.

His brother read that he had to take a course in humanities, and his younger brother announced, *"I kissed a manatee, once!"*

##

I always love shopping with the kids because they get silly and continue to amaze me. At least they're well behaved and make everyone laugh, instead of cringe.

##

I was on my way out to a local discount store one afternoon when he asked to come with me. We made our way to the electronics section, where we split up.

He started whining (from a different aisle), *"Mom! Mom!"*

I walked over to him and asked what he wanted.

"Buy me a remote! I need a remote! I don't have a remote in my bedroom."

By now, everyone in the department was watching us because I was laughing and this 16-year-old was carrying on. Hopefully they realized that he was kidding.

He continued with, *"But Mom! When I want to change the channel, I have to <u>roll over</u>."*

More recently, he accompanied my daughter and me when she needed a special outfit. I was looking for knee socks or pantyhose appropriate for her to wear under slacks. At the same time, both of them spotted an item called, *Trouser Socks*, which was exactly what I was looking for.

They laughed at the name of the product and were giggling and having fun. Most of the other (older) shoppers around us were having a wonderful time watching them. I had to admit that I didn't take them shopping together often, and this was why.

Then, a short time later, he called us with his cell phone from a remote corner of the store because he couldn't find us while we were near the fitting rooms.

I received a phone call from his high school French teacher who was, *"unhappy with his attitude in class."*

I asked what he was doing and if he was being disrespectful, and she assured me that he was not. Apparently, when she had asked him why he was taking French, he had answered, *"to get into college."*

She was expecting an answer similar to *"Because I love the language."*

I told her I would address the issue if he was being disrespectful, but that he was only being honest.

##

He selected college locations based on the fishing conditions of the area, but ended up staying within the state.

##

After he had locked his keys in his car for the third time, I brought a coat hanger to teach him the trick that all new drivers eventually learn about *breaking into* their own cars.

"Wow! That's great," he said, *"I'm going to keep [the bent hanger] in my trunk in case I lock my keys inside again!"*

##

He completed his sophomore project a week before graduation; his senior project was submitted two days later.

Theoretically, he was a high school senior for approximately three days prior to graduation.

##

Interestingly enough, shortly after graduation, four of his teachers *and* the Principal announced their retirement.

Coincidence? We think not.

##

When he was involved in his first accident, the police dispatcher contacted the parents of everyone involved.

Apparently, if I couldn't been contacted by phone, the officer at the scene would have driven him home.

I received the call from the dispatcher informing me that my son had been involved in an accident; he wasn't hurt, but I needed to go to the scene immediately.

As we raced to dress, I woke his sister to contact his father, and headed to the address a quarter-mile away.

My mind was racing and I was swearing under my breath, praying he wasn't injured, hoping no one else was hurt, and wondering about the insurance consequences, etc.

When I arrived at the scene, I surveyed the surroundings. I saw a green van, a bunch of people standing around on the side of the road, and a police cruiser with lights—but no white car. I thought the car went over the embankment.

After I parked and walked first to look over the embankment (no car) and then to the police cruiser, I introduced myself to the officer. He shook my hand and asked what *he* could do for *me*.

It turns out my son had nothing to do with the accident —he was just a passenger in the van and was unhurt.

He had apparently spoken to the officer and asked that, if he had to be brought home, could he be placed in handcuffs.

He told the policeman, *"If my mom thinks I caused an accident, I'll be safer in your custody than I will be in hers."*

##

When he was a young teen, I teased him that one of these days he'd wake up and be very tall, covered with hair and zits, and working at a fast-food restaurant.

I said, we'll pull up to the window and you'll say, "Do you want fries with that?"

He promptly responded, "and you'll be at the window answering, "Did I *ask* for fries?"

##

During his first year at college, he was home seven out of the first ten weekends. Apparently he wasn't completely comfortable with the term "going away" to college.

##

Together We Are a Happy Family

(God Help Us)

The rest of these are self-explanatory. They're not all funny, but they did all happen. Hopefully, you'll see your children in here, somewhere.

From the time the boys were very young, I always scheduled their doctor appointments together. In most circumstances, one was hyperactive and one was (a bit) quieter while the doctor was performing his checkups.

When the boys were one and four, I had professional pictures taken. They looked adorable, and I sent a wallet-sized print to their doctor, who posted it on his patient bulletin board amongst the others.

He remarked one day that every time he entered the room for the exam, he stopped to look at that picture. He said the boys are adorable, but there was an evil twinkle in the younger one's eye that only a doctor (or parent) would notice.

He and I both knew that this child was so adorable that he could get away with almost anything, because he could crawl into someone's lap and look and act like an angel.

He is the one who later convinced his six-year-old brother to jump down a flight of stairs.

Personally, I think it was payback for his brother "feeding him" a penny when he (the younger son) was three months old.

When his brother was four, he wrote all over the couch with a green magic marker and tried to convince us that the one-year-old had accomplished this feat. Never mind the fact that we *saw him* shove the marker into his hand when he heard us coming.

The boys were five and seven when they came running from the bus stop and down our 200-foot driveway yelling, *"Mom! Mom!"*

When I calmed them down, they excitedly asked, *"Is Papa a virgin?"*

I asked them to repeat their question (wondering where they might have heard the term), and I started laughing when they explained, *"You know, was he in a war?"*

SPECIAL DISCOUNT FOR
WWII VIRGINS

##

It was holiday season, I was pregnant and tired, and the boys (ages three and four) hadn't eaten. I was waiting at the checkout of a discount department store full of customers at about 6:30 p.m. in the middle of winter.

They were cranky, noisy, arguing with each other, and carrying on in the cart. They started pulling candy off the shelves and became those terrible children all shoppers hate.

From behind clenched teeth, I threatened under my breath, *"If you don't behave, I'm going to take you into the parking lot and beat you up!"*

There was obviously no fear that I would actually carry out such a threat, and the older woman in front of me actually cracked a smile.

Then my oldest said, *"Wow! Can I beat him up, too?"*

##

It's great that we have these wonderful memories to look back on, and we do—often, when we are together. There's nothing I love more than a houseful of laughter.

It's even more fun when their friends are over! The very fact that my kids can laugh at themselves and each other is something they will enjoy their entire lives.

When the boys were young, they wanted to visit Universal Studios to see their favorite cartoon characters _live_.

The concept was so funny because years earlier, their father proclaimed, _"Jurassic Park" to be "the most realistic movie [he'd] ever seen."_ I had then asked, _"When is the last time you saw a dinosaur?"_

One night, all three kids and a group of friends were playing Jeopardy on the video game system. I was walking upstairs when they were excitingly asking each other, _"Who recorded the Twist?"_

One of the friends turned and asked me, and I answered, _"Chubby Checker."_

They all laughed because they were sure I had made up the answer, but when they entered it, they were surprised to learn I was right. At their request, I kept playing for both teams until we were all tired of laughing and competing.

##

I truly believe in the quote from Dick Clark, *"Music Is the Soundtrack to Your Life."*

##

The whole family loves music, but different genres. We took the boys to see the Monkees in concert when they were three and five because they loved watching reruns of the original 1960s show on Nickelodeon. We even have a video recording of the Monkees[7] singing Happy Birthday to our 5-year-old from a local TV call-in show that I called the afternoon of the concert.

By the time the group finally appeared on stage at 10 p.m., the boys were less than enthusiastic, but our intentions were good.

[7]*reference to The Monkees band and TV show originally aired in 1966*

##

When the boys were a little older, the Beach Boys were opening for David Cassidy at a local venue. I made a big deal about the concert—because the kids knew a lot of Beach Boys songs—but as soon as we got there, they recognized my mission and said, *"We're only here because you wanted to see David Cassidy!"*[8] (They were right.)

[8]*reference to the lead singer of the Partridge Family TV show originally aired in 1970*

##

My oldest son was afraid of heights and was hypersensitive to loud noises. Little did I know that the seats I got to a sold-out Garth Brooks concert for his 12th birthday were at the top of the stands—just over the speakers.

It took him a while, but soon he was comfortable enough to enjoy his favorite singer and the whole concert experience.

He was also thrilled to learn that he had stood near Garth's parents in line at the concession stand.

At the end of the concert, when the entire audience sang along to *American Pie*[9]*,* he wanted to know how everyone knew the words, because Garth had just started singing it. He didn't know that Don MacLean sang it when I was in high school.

[9]reference to *American Pie* by Don MacLean in 1971

To this day, I have no idea why my generation is so fascinated with that song, or why almost everyone knows the lyrics. I remember in high school and afterwards, waiting in the car for the song to finish—whether we were going to a restaurant, the mall, or a movie.

It was probably as popular as *"Paradise by the Dashboard Light."*[10]

[10]reference to *Paradise by the Dashboard Light* by Meatloaf in 1977

##

The two youngest (ages 10 and 7 at the time) claimed not to share the same passion for country music that my oldest son and I enjoyed.

But when Garth Brooks' *Friends in Low Places*[11] came on the radio, *all four* of us sang along and it was obvious that we *all* knew the words.

[11]reference to *Friends in Low Places* by Garth Brooks in 1994

I was watching a group on the Tonight Show[12], but I had missed their name when they were announced. I asked my younger son, *"Who are: Something Something and the Something Something Somethings?"* and he knew instantly that it was Voodoo Daddy and the Big Bad Voodoo Daddies.

[12]reference to the Tonight Show with Jay Leno on October 22, 1999

When the oldest was studying Spanish in high school, I gave him a cassette tape of Marc Anthony. I didn't realize that one side was in Spanish and the other was in English.

I asked him to bring the tape to school so his teacher could translate, because I wanted to know the words of my new favorite song.

He looked at both sides of the tape and handed it back to me saying, *"Mom—just turn it over!"*

##

My daughter misheard the lyrics of *Lady Marmalade*[13,14] from the *Moulin Rouge* soundtrack, not knowing it was originally recorded in the 1970's.

She heard *"Creole Lady..."* as *"Three Old Ladies..."* and thought the song was about elderly prostitutes.

[13]reference to *Moulin Rouge* soundtrack 2001
[14]reference to *Lady Marmalade* single by Labelle 1976

She has told her friends, *"My mom has the soundtrack to everything."*

My youngest son ran around the house singing *I'm a Dancing Queen*[15] when he was 14; he didn't realize it was a relatively old song. [15]reference to *Dancing Queen* by Abba in 1976

He also thought *Queen*[16] was a new band, too. I explained that lead singer, Freddie Mercury, was dead and the tribute band had already toured. [16]reference to *Queen* formed in 1970

##

My daughter liked disco and went through an *I Will Survive*[17] and *It's Raining Men*[18] period before she discovered Kenny Rogers.

She began obsessing on every other song of his Greatest Hits[19] album and pre-programmed the CD player in my car to repeat the songs over, and over, and over, until her brothers hid the CD.

[17]reference to *I Will Survive* by Gloria Gainer in 1978
[18]reference to *It's Raining Men* by The Weather Girls in 1982
[19]reference to *Kenny Rogers Greatest Hits* album released in 1980

A few years back, I found a stereo system at a yard sale for $15. It was in perfect condition, complete with receiver, speakers, turntable and a new needle cartridge. I set it up and went to Goodwill to buy a few records for 49¢ each.

At home, we hooked everything up to show the kids the pleasure of listening to vinyl albums.

They were absolutely amazed and wanted to know how to rewind the album, because they wanted to listen to a song again.

I got up, lifted the needle to the correct track, set it back down, placed the plastic cover over the turntable, and we listened to the same song again.

##

It wasn't bad enough that my kids hadn't heard of the groups we were listening to (*Air Supply*[20] and *The Police*[21]), but when they heard *Every Breath You Take*[22], they all thought it was a *remake* of a Puff Daddy[23] recording.

[20]reference to *Air Supply* formed in 1980
[21]reference to *The Police* formed in 1977
[22]reference to *Every Breath You Take* by the Police in 1983
[23]reference to *Every Breath You Take* by Puff Daddy in 1997

##

When the boys were little, their sitter thought it was *awesome* that my husband and I had all the Beatles albums.[24] I had to explain that we didn't buy them all at once, we bought them as they were released.

She also wanted to know if Paul McCartney was in any other band before Wings.[25] Ouch!

[24]reference to approximately 25 Beatles albums from 1965—1977
[25]reference to the formation of the band Wings by Paul McCartney in 1971.

##

Then again, my daughter saw Paul McCartney on a recent television commercial and asked, *"Paul McCartney—isn't he someone famous? Weren't there more Beatles?"*

##

Sometimes, we just take things for granted. When my oldest son told me that he was asked a question about "Smokey Bear" on his college final exam, I was surprised.

Not only was a surprised, but I was amazed that he answered

the question incorrectly. However, thinking back on the actual question posed, I wondered how many people could have answered correctly.

He was asked "What does Smokey Bear carry?" While it is obvious once you see the sign that he carries a shovel, my son answered "fire rake."

From my son's point of view, a shovel wasn't a fire-fighting implement. I teased him (often), and had a picture of Smokey put on his 18th birthday cake which was served at Boy Scout Camp (which uses Smokey as a logo throughout the site). We also sent up gifts of shovels, pails, and a Smokey Bear baseball cap.

I suggested the camp give him questions about fire safety in the guise of a party game. Across the bottom of the cake I had the word "Gotcha" written, and then teasing ending on that day. (See reference to Gotcha on the next page.)

##

One of [my] favorite things I started with the kids was the *"Gotcha."* They, on the other hand, usually don't like it. This is a way to remind them I'm there, whether they like it or not, and suggests that I am watching over their shoulders, like their conscience.

It is also a way to say *I Love You,* or *Surprise!* depending on the circumstance or occasion. Whatever happens, I acknowledge my presence by signing or printing the word *Gotcha* on a card, gift, cake, etc.

Gotcha's have included a baby picture on a 16th birthday cake, balloons delivered to school for a birthday, arranging for my ex-father-in-law to present my son's Eagle Scout honor (no "Gotcha" card was needed in this instance), planning a surprise party at Boy Scout Camp, etc. The boys know I've had their backs, at least in a few situations.

My daughter earned her first *Gotcha* when I arranged for her (my) favorite baby picture to be printed in her high school yearbook this year with a congratulatory graduation message. At my son's prompting, I didn't include her name because, as he said, "Everyone will know it's her."

According to my daughter, they did. And she liked the picture.

##

While my son was a Boy Scout, close to qualifying for his Eagle Scout designation, we were having a discussion about flag etiquette.

It was his belief that etiquette was not the law; I, on the other hand, believed there to be laws governing the care and maintenance of the United States flag.

One of my concerns was a neighbor that had constructed a large flag pole; the flag was left flying at night, and I was understood that the flag must be illuminated if flown outside after sundown.

According to the United States Code, Chapter 1, Title 4, Section 6 entitled, "Patriotic Customs," I knew that, "…it is the universal custom to display the flag only from sunrise to sunset on buildings and on stationary flagstaffs in the open. However…, the flag may be displayed twenty-four hours a day if properly illuminated during the hours of darkness."

My son countered with, "The Flag Code is intended as a guide to be followed on a purely voluntary basis to insure proper respect for the flag."

We both ended up laughing when he said, "Mom, trust me. No one has even been put in prison for not illuminating their flag." I don't know if that's true or not, but the quote was wonderfully amusing at the time.

##

When the kids were young, they suffered from what the pediatrician called "Tactile sensitivity." They didn't want sheets on their beds, my daughter preferred to be wrapped in a towel than a blanket, and the oldest insisted on being tightly swaddled in a warm blanket, even in the heat of August.

In fact, a woman in a department store scolded me for keeping him too warmly wrapped up; so, I unwrapped him and he started to scream as she stood there and watched. Then, I swiftly rewrapped him and he calmed instantly. She walked away shaking her head, and didn't even apologize for being so rude.

##

A woman walked up to me in the grocery store and looked at the two boys in the cart. They were a year-and-a-half and three years old. One was blonde, the other dark-haired, and the woman scoffed, "*Those children obviously had different fathers.*"

My husband and I later thought we should have said, "No, they had different mothers."

##

I showed up at home eating chocolate covered raisins, and he boys (about 3 and 4) ran to ask where I got them. I told them they were out in the woods and pointed to an area on the far side of the yard.

I had my husband keep them looking while I ran around the

corner and picked up several bags at the convenience store.

When I returned, I found a section of the yard that they hadn't inspected yet and scattered the bags under bushes and trees. When they finally found their treats, we heard screams of delight, which, as far as I was concerned, was well worth the effort.

Bear in mind that a year later, these boys would come out of the same woods carrying two of the largest box turtles I had ever seen (from the wetlands behind our yard).

##

When the kids were much younger, friends of ours adopted a kitten but had to give it up because she cried—constantly. When we arrived for a visit, they thrust her at us. We felt bad, and reluctantly took her to join our household of critters.

During the entire 12-mile ride, she cried—and cried, and cried. It was not a cute kitten cry, but a wailing, pitiful cry.

Once we got her home and set her on the ground to explore her new surroundings, she stopped crying. In fact, she rarely cried at all after that. The next morning, the children were concerned because they heard a cat meowing.

They accounted for each of the cats in our household, one by one, but still didn't know about the new one.

Finally, my youngest son pulled the kitten from the couch (it had crawled under the sofa, and was confused or trapped underneath) and exclaimed, *"Who's this?"*

I told the kids that when they sat on the couch, it made a kitten!

##

Recent Family Portrait

Update

As of summer 2007, my oldest son graduated Unity College with a Bachelor of Science degree in Conservation Law Enforcement in 2006 and is a seasonal member of the Old Orchard Beach [Maine] Police Department.

##

His younger brother is entering his senior year at the University of NH and is pursuing an education and career in Mechanical Engineering.

##

In 2006 and 2007, my daughter entered and won several statewide competitions. She graduated high school with art awards and scholarships and was voted one of the high school's "most artistic" students.

She is leaving soon to pursue a degree in Illustration at Boston College of Art. Someday, we'll all be able to view her creativity in galleries (or comic books) around the world.

Her guidance counselor and I decided that she'd be president one day, although her counselor added, *"Hopefully, it will be for a friendly country."*

##

www.ingramcontent.com/pod-product-compliance
Lightning Source LLC
Chambersburg PA
CBHW022028090426
42739CB00006BA/335